MW01077837

# ESTHER

## TRUSTING
## GOD'S PLAN

A Bible study based
on the teaching of

———

NANCY DeMOSS
WOLGEMUTH

Published by *Revive Our Hearts*
P.O. Box 2000, Niles, MI 49120

ISBN: 978-1-934718-71-1

Printed in the United States of America.

Adapted from the teaching of Nancy DeMoss Wolgemuth by Paula Marsteller, Mindy Kroesche, and Leslie Bennett, edited by Hayley Mullins and Erin Davis.

All Scripture quotations are from the ESV® Bible (The Holy Bible, English Standard Version®), copyright © 2001 by Crossway, a publishing ministry of Good News Publishers. Used by permission. All rights reserved.

As you work through this study, use this space to doodle, color, and meditate on God's Word and consider how the book of Esther gives you true hope.

FOR WHATEVER WAS WRITTEN IN FORMER DAYS WAS WRITTEN FOR OUR INSTRUCTION THAT THROUGH endurance & THROUGH THE encouragement OF THE Scriptures WE MIGHT HAVE hope. ROMANS 15:4

# Esther's story

## AS IT BEGINS IN ESTHER 1

[1] Now in the days of Ahasuerus, the Ahasuerus who reigned from India to Ethiopia over 127 provinces, [2] in those days when King Ahasuerus sat on his royal throne in Susa, the citadel, [3] in the third year of his reign he gave a feast for all his officials and servants. The army of Persia and Media and the nobles and governors of the provinces were before him, [4] while he showed the riches of his royal glory and the splendor and pomp of his greatness for many days, 180 days.

[5] And when these days were completed, the king gave for all the people present in Susa the citadel, both great and small, a feast lasting for seven days in the court of the garden of the king's palace. [6] There were white cotton curtains and violet hangings fastened with cords of fine linen and purple to silver rods and marble pillars, and also couches of gold and silver on a mosaic pavement of porphyry, marble, mother-of-pearl, and precious stones.

[7] Drinks were served in golden vessels, vessels of different kinds, and the royal wine was lavished according to the bounty of the king. [8] And drinking was according to this edict: "There is no compulsion." For the king had given orders to all the staff of his palace to do as each man desired. [9] Queen Vashti also gave a feast for the women in the palace that belonged to King Ahasuerus.

¹⁰ On the seventh day, when the heart of the king was merry with wine, he commanded Mehuman, Biztha, Harbona, Bigtha and Abagtha, Zethar and Carkas, the seven eunuchs who served in the presence of King Ahasuerus, ¹¹ to bring Queen Vashti before the king with her royal crown, in order to show the peoples and the princes her beauty, for she was lovely to look at. ¹² But Queen Vashti refused to come at the king's command delivered by the eunuchs. At this the king became enraged, and his anger burned within him.

¹³ Then the king said to the wise men who knew the times (for this was the king's procedure toward all who were versed in law and judgment, ¹⁴ the men next to him being Carshena, Shethar, Admatha, Tarshish, Meres, Marsena, and Memucan, the seven princes of Persia and Media, who saw the king's face, and sat first in the kingdom):

¹⁵ "According to the law, what is to be done to Queen Vashti, because she has not performed the command of King Ahasuerus delivered by the eunuchs?" ¹⁶ Then Memucan said in the presence of the king and the officials, "Not only against the king has Queen Vashti done wrong, but also against all the officials and all the peoples who are in all the provinces of King Ahasuerus.

¹⁷ For the queen's behavior will be made known to all women, causing them to look at their husbands with contempt, since they will say, 'King Ahasuerus commanded Queen Vashti to be brought before him, and she did not come.' ¹⁸ This very day the noble women of Persia and Media who have heard of the queen's behavior will say the same to all the king's officials, and there will be contempt and wrath in plenty.

¹⁹ If it please the king, let a royal order go out from him, and let it be written among the laws of the Persians and the Medes so that it may not be repealed, that Vashti is never again to come before King Ahasuerus. And let the king give her royal position to another who is better than she. ²⁰ So when the decree made by the king is proclaimed throughout all his kingdom, for it is vast, all women will give honor to their husbands, high and low alike." ²¹ This advice pleased the king and the princes, and the king did as Memucan proposed. ²² He sent letters to all the royal provinces, to every province in its own script and to every people in its own language, that every man be master in his own household and speak according to the language of his people.

It may be safer to look through your windshield when you're driving, but glancing in your rearview mirror gives you a clear look at where you've been. God's providence is often better seen in retrospect than in the moment.

The Old Testament book of Esther makes no reference to God, but the entire story bears the unmistakable imprint of His ways. God will strengthen your faith as you see how He intervened to deliver His people. The Lord *still* masterfully orchestrates every detail of our lives and this universe in jaw-dropping ways. Nothing and no one can thwart His plan!

Expect these seven truths to deeply embed themselves in your heart through this study:

- **You are in a battle.**
- **God has a sovereign plan.**
- **You are a part of God's plan.**
- **God's plan will never fail.**
- **It's a beautiful thing to live under God's caring providence.**
- **There is no situation so desperate God cannot redeem it.**
- **Don't judge the outcome of the battle by the way things look right now.**

TIPS FOR USING THIS STUDY

Throughout this study, ask yourself:

- What does this passage teach me about the heart, ways, and character of God?
- How does this passage point to Jesus and the gospel?
- Is there an example to follow or avoid? If so, how should I seek to change in response?

Each week of study is divided into five suggested daily lessons, but feel free to work at your own pace. Do what works for you!

As you go through the study, you may find it beneficial to listen to the audio series "Esther: God's Woman at God's Time." Find it at ReviveOurHearts.com/Esther-Series.

Remember, the Holy Spirit is our primary teacher as we seek to understand God's Word. Jesus told us that the Holy Spirit is a gift and a "Helper" able to "teach you all things and bring to your remembrance all that I have said to you" (John 14:26).

Secondary tools that can help you better understand the Word of God (but aren't necessary to complete this study) include:

- An English dictionary to look up the basic meaning of words
- Various translations of the Bible
- A concordance
- A Bible dictionary
- Commentaries
- A study Bible
- Colored pens or pencils to write in your Bible.

Note: Throughout this study, you will find fill-in-the-blank sections using the English Standard Version (ESV) translation of the Bible. If you prefer a different translation, you can use an online Bible such as BibleGateway.com or a Bible app to help with these sections.

We've also included group discussion questions at the end of this study. You can further join the Esther discussion with our Women of the Bible podcast created to accompany this study, available at ReviveOurHearts.com.

OUR HOPE FOR YOU

During the next six weeks, may God:

- Grow your awareness and trust in His providence.
- Expand your humility as you wait on His perfect timing.
- Bear the fruit of self-control and restraint in your life.

He is faithful to do it.

Spend time meditating on and memorizing the following verse this week:

the KING'S heart is a stream of water in the HAND of the Lord; he turns it WHEREVER he will

PROVERBS 21:1

# Week 1

GOD SETS THE STAGE

As we look back over history, we can often see God's hand directing events. Joseph was sold into slavery by his brothers, thrown in jail for a crime he didn't commit ... putting him in the position to interpret Pharaoh's dream, become second-in-command over Egypt, and ultimately save the Egyptian people and his own family (Gen. 50:20).

The persecution of the early church in Jerusalem had believers running for their lives (Acts 8:1) ... resulting in the spread of the gospel across the Roman Empire. In more recent times, the weather report for June 6, 1944 had German officials believing there could be no attack ... leaving their troops unprepared and opened the way for the Allied Forces' invasion on D-Day. [4]

At the time of these events, those involved probably didn't see God at work. Esther, Mordecai, and the Jewish people in the Persian Empire may have wondered if He was working too. Living under the rule of a tyrannical king, it would have been difficult to see God in their circumstances. But as we find out in this week's study, even when we can't see His hand, we can trust that God is working for our good and His glory.

## Day 1: Meet the Cast:
THE INVISIBLE HAND

*Read Esther 1.*

## Before the Curtain Goes Up

About 100 years before Esther's story begins in 586 B.C., the Jews were taken captive to Babylon as God's discipline for their sin (Jer. 52). They were captives in Babylon for seventy years before the Babylonian Empire fell to the Persians (Jer. 29:10). God then worked through King Cyrus (Ezra 1:1–6) to give the Jews the freedom to return to their homeland (around 538 B.C.). However, many stayed behind in Persia, including Mordecai and Esther's families.[1]

At its height, the Persian Empire was vast, spanning from the Balkan Peninsula—including parts of what is present day Bulgaria, Romania, and Ukraine—to modern-day India and all the way south to Egypt.[2] Our story takes place in this empire, in the city of Susa (located in modern-day Iran).[3] The curtain goes up on the story of Esther about 450 years before the promised Messiah would be born.

The story of Esther is an account of God intervening in history to deliver His chosen people from annihilation. Why was it so important to the fulfillment of God's promises and plan that the Jewish people not be destroyed? (Look for clues in the two passages below.)

_____

_____

## 1. Read Genesis 3:15

Theologians recognize this as the first gospel proclamation in all of Scripture.

Who do you think the "woman's offspring" is referring to? Who would eventually bruise Satan's head? What answer do we find in Galatians 4:4–5?

_____

_____

## 2. Read Genesis 22:18

Centuries before Esther came on the scene, God promised Abraham, "In your _____ shall _____ of the earth be blessed."

Galatians 3:8 tells us that this promise to Abraham was another gospel proclamation. Write out the verse below.

_____

_____

_____

Galatians 3:16 goes on to clearly state who Abraham's offspring would be:

> Now the promises were made to Abraham and to his offspring.
> It does not say, "And to offsprings," referring to many,
> but referring to one, "And to your offspring," who is Christ.

In the book of Esther, we see God preserving the Jewish nation so the Messiah could still come from Abraham.

# *Esther's story is really God's story.*

As you read the book of Esther, you will see God's:

- *Faithfulness* to His covenant and His people.
- *Sovereign control* over every circumstance.
- *Providence.*

How would you define the providence of God?

_____

_____

## God's Mysterious, Interesting Providence

Professor Dale Ralph Davis refers to God's providence as "that frequently mysterious, always interesting way in which Yahweh provides for his servants in their various needs." [5] Start looking for God's providence, and you'll see it everywhere!

You'll see in Esther that God has a plan that cannot be thwarted by anything. God *will* deliver His people and ultimately fulfill all His purposes in this world. May this story from Scripture help you recognize the unseen hand of God that's always at work in your life.

If someone wrote an account of the "coincidences" in your life, what are some stories they might include of God's providence at work?

_____

_____

_____

Even when you can't see it, God is there. His work is hidden from our sight many times, but He is always acting on behalf of His people and His glory. The book of Esther is a beautiful portrayal of Romans 8:28.

Look it up, and then personalize it with your name:

> And we know that for _____ all things work together for good, for
> those who _____ are called according to his purpose.

This incredible story helps us marvel at the masterful way God orchestrates every detail of our lives and of this universe. When you cannot see the hand of God, trust His heart and know that His providence is always working on your behalf.

Take a few moments to write out a prayer asking God to give you eyes to see His providence working over the next few weeks.

_____

_____

_____

_____

_____

# Day 2: *Meet the Cast:*
## KING XERXES

*Read Esther 1:1–8.*

Depending on your Bible translation, you might see "Ahasuerus" or "Xerxes" in the first verse of Esther. This is one and the same man. Ahasuerus is his Persian title, meaning "high father" or "venerable king"; and his Greek name is "Xerxes the Great." (We'll use Xerxes in this study, since it's easier to pronounce.)

At the time of Esther, King Xerxes was one of the most powerful men on the face of the earth. He reigned from 486 to 465 B.C. over a world empire.

The story of Esther begins as Xerxes hosts a lavish feast. Who was this feast for and why did he give it (vv. 3–4)?

_____

_____

According to verse 4, how long was the feast? _____ days (That's a six-month-long party!)

Many think Xerxes gave this feast to gain support for—and prove he had the resources for—a war he was preparing to wage against the Greeks.

This six-month feast climaxes in a massive banquet for

_____, lasting _____ days (v. 5).

He didn't skimp on this banquet either! Describe the party setting (v. 6).

_____

_____

_____

Scripture records that alcohol was a part of the party atmosphere (vv. 7–8). The drinking was according to what edict?

_____

_____

_____

A Persian law stated that every time the king took a drink, the people had to take a drink. He probably didn't want people to feel like they had to drink every time he did, so he waived that law for this feast.

What wisdom does Proverbs 31:4–5 give?

_____

*About the Wine . . .*

The Bible makes clear that the *abuse* of alcohol is to be avoided (see, for example, Eph. 5:18). But believers in the church disagree on specifics. Some focus on the potential dangers of drinking (Prov. 20:1, 23:29–30), while others point out that wine is a gift from God intended for our enjoyment (Ps. 104:14–15; Isa. 55:1; John 2:1–11).

Christians have freedom in this matter. To take one position does not necessarily make us more spiritual than if we take

# Three Snapshots of the Man Esther Married

We learn what sort of ruler Xerxes was from the Greek historian, Herodotus. These graphic images tell the story of an erratic king.

SNAPSHOT 1: A man named Pythias offered Xerxes an enormous sum of money to wage war against the Greeks. When Pythias asked Xerxes if just one of his sons could stay home instead of going to war, Xerxes had that son cut in half and made his whole army pass between the pieces of the severed body. [7]

SNAPSHOT 2: When a storm destroyed the two bridges Xerxes' men had built across the Hellespont, he had the engineers beheaded and the water beaten with 300 lashes.[8]

SNAPSHOT 3: At one point, Xerxes tried to seduce his brother's wife. When she refused him, he had an affair with her daughter and then arranged for her whole family to be murdered. [9]

another. But neither do we have a license to tear down those who disagree with us. Here are several questions that are helpful in determining our practice in this matter—as well as in other potentially enslaving behaviors:

1. Is it harming my body?
2. Does it—or could it—enslave me?
3. Is alcohol an idol in my life?
4. Could my drinking cause spiritual damage to others or lead them into sin? [6]

For more on this topic, check out chapter 7 in *Adorned: Living Out the Beauty of the Gospel Together.*

## Don't Lose Hope

Do you know any angry, cruel, and vindictive people like Xerxes?

You might have grown up with, married, or worked for someone like this. In His providence, God sometimes allows ungodly people to be in charge. When this happens, it's easy to lose hope or think nothing will ever be different.

But remember, the final chapter hasn't been written yet. The success of the ungodly is short-lived. God overrules even the orders of wicked men because He is _____ _____ (find the answer in Psalm 47:7).

King Xerxes' pride becomes a set-up for God to demonstrate His power and His kingdom, which rules over all kings and kingdoms of this earth.

You may not be under the authority of a cruel, vindictive king, but we all know how it feels to be impacted by someone whose actions are ungodly or unfair. Journal about a time when you were under such authority. (Maybe that time is now.) Can you see evidence of the Lord's hand? Write about that, too.

_____

_____

_____

_____

_____

# Day 3: *Meet the Cast:*

*Read Esther 1:9–12.*

We're now introduced to another character in this cast: Queen Vashti. When we meet her, she is fulfilling her role as the queen. According to Esther 1:9, what was she doing?

_____

_____

The feasting and banquets in those days would have been segregated. It would have gone against protocol for the women to come into the place where men were feasting. Yet what does the king command in verses 10 –11?

_____

_____

Why does he request this (v. 11)?

_____

After six months of arrogant show-and-tell, under the influence of alcohol, King Xerxes decides to show off the one thing he hasn't yet shown off—his queen. But Queen Vashti
_____ (v. 12).

Do you think Vashti did the right thing in defying her husband's order? Why or why not?

_____

_____

We don't know exactly *why* Vashti refused to come or *how* she refused to come. That raises the question: Is it ever right to disobey those in authority over us? What do you think and why?

_____

_____

_____

_____

*Read Romans 13:1-5.*

God's Word is clear that He has ordained authority and that we are to submit to it. However, the exception seems to be when authority encourages us to break one of God's commands. Look up the following verses. Then circle whether you think the actions of the people in these examples were pleasing to God and why.

EXODUS 1:16-17, 20

Yes/No

*Explain your answer:*

_____

_____

_____

DANIEL 3:16-18

Yes/No

*Explain your answer:*

_____

_____

_____

DANIEL 6:7, 10

Yes/No

*Explain your answer:*

_____

_____

_____

ACTS 4:16-17, 20

Yes/No

*Explain your answer:*

_____

_____

_____

ACTS 5:27-32

Yes/No

*Explain your answer:*

_____

_____

_____

God used Vashti's situation to position Esther in the palace "for such a time as this." In God's providence, He overruled a tragic situation for the good of His people and the fulfillment of His redemptive plan.

God is able to overrule even the worst situation for your good and the fulfillment of His plan. How have you seen Him do this in the past?

_____

_____

How are you hoping for God's providence to intervene in a current situation? Write it out as a prayer below.

_____

_____

_____

_____

_____

## Day 4: *Meet the Cast:*
### THE KING'S ADVISORS

*Read Esther 1:12–22.*

How did King Xerxes respond when his queen didn't come (Est. 1:12)?

_____

_____

Perhaps the king was used to getting everything he wanted . . . until this moment. He had just been disrespected in front of the very people he's spent six months trying to impress. So he turned to his wise men for advice. Read verses 13–14.

How many men did the king consult, and who were they?

_____

_____

In verse 15, what wrong does Xerxes accuse Vashti of?

_____

_____

Whom did Memucan say the queen had wronged (v. 16)? Do you think this is an exaggeration? Why or why not?

_____

_____

What was Memucan concerned would happen once other women in the kingdom heard about Vashti's behavior (v. 17–18)?

_____

_____

How did Memucan advise the king in verse 19? Do you think his counsel was good? Why or why not?

_____

_____

Memucan gave King Xerxes earthly wisdom. James 3:13–18 contrasts this kind of "wisdom" with the wisdom that is from above. According to this passage, what characterizes true wisdom?

_____

_____

What did the king think of Memucan's advice (Est. 1:21–22), and what did he do in response? As a woman, how do you feel about the way Vashti was treated?

_____

_____

We see that God's purposes were set in motion, even through Xerxes' ungodly choices. What did Xerxes' treatment of Vashti set the stage for?

_____

_____

As you walk into the next lessons, notice this detail from verse 19: The law of the Persians and the Medes was a law that couldn't be reversed, even by the king. Apparently the people felt it was better to be ruled by kings who made rash laws, as long as they couldn't then change those laws.

Practice this week's memory verse, Proverbs 21:1, by writing it out and placing it somewhere prominent, such as your bathroom mirror or car steering wheel.

## Day 5: Meet the Cast:
### THE HERO OF THE STORY

*Re-read Esther 1.*

Write out John 10:10 below.

_____

_____

_____

_____

According to this verse, what is Satan's goal? What is God's goal?

_____

_____

_____

We can trust that though Satan seeks to kill and destroy, God came to give us abundant life. The Old Testament is filled with story after story of Satan trying to destroy the people of God so the Messiah could not be born and God gaining the victory over his devices. Name a couple of examples you can think of.

_____

_____

_____

In the book of Esther, the people of God are once again under attack. The Jewish race faces extermination, chiefly through one powerful man named Haman. (We'll learn more about him in future chapters.)

As you read the book of Esther, watch for this thread: There's a battle between the kingdom of man and the kingdom of God. In this story, King Xerxes and Haman represent the kingdom of man. Mordecai and Esther represent the kingdom of God.

That's not to say Mordecai and Esther were perfect; they definitely had their flaws. But they also seem to have a heart for God. However, at the end of the day, Esther and Mordecai are not the heroes of this story. *God is.*

As you begin your journey through Esther, write down some differences between the kingdom of man and the kingdom of God, using the prompts below.

### The Kingdom of Man Versus the Kingdom of God

The kingdom of man is visible. The kingdom of God is _____ (2 Cor. 4:18).

The kingdom of man is a kingdom of darkness. God's kingdom is a kingdom of _____ (1 Peter 2:9).

The kingdom of man is temporal. But the kingdom of God is _____. It will never be overthrown (Dan. 7:13–14).

Which of these truths encourages your heart the most today and why?

_____

_____

_____

_____

It's challenging for us—as it was in Esther's day—to live as children of God in a world that doesn't recognize Him as King. What temporary things are most likely to distract you from investing in God's invisible, eternal kingdom? List them below.

_____

_____

_____

_____

Spend time meditating on and memorizing the following verse this week:

He will not let your foot be MOVED; he who keeps you will not SLUMBER.

PSALM 121:3

## "A Gentle and Quiet Spirit"

by Mary Kassian

"Most translations [of 1 Peter 3:4–6] use the word *quiet* to describe this attitude of serenity and tranquility. Being calm means being settled, firm, immovable, steadfast, and peaceful in spirit. A calm disposition is like a still, peaceful pool of water, as opposed to a churning whirlpool that's agitated and stirred up . . .

According to the Bible, a calm spirit goes hand in hand with trusting the Lord [see Isa. 30:15]. God's love quiets us and is the source of our calm (Zeph. 3:17) . . . Quietness has more to do with the state of our hearts than the quantity and volume of our words (although the one definitely influences the other). Even women who are gregarious, extroverted, and sociable can achieve a calm, tranquil spirit." [10]

# Week 2

## A NEW QUEEN IS CROWNED

We all know women in our circle of influence who are in tough circumstances:

- Difficult marriages
- Strained family relationships
- Difficult work environments
- Ongoing health difficulties

That woman might even be you!

When we go through tough times, it's easy to feel as if God has forgotten us—and let that feeling dictate our reactions. But as we see in this week's study, even in the worst of circumstances, a woman of God can grow in favor with God and others if she has a winsome spirit and godly character. God works through our lives to accomplish His purposes, just as He did in Esther's life.

## Day 1: *An Ugly Beauty Contest*

*Read Esther 2.*

History tells us King Xerxes didn't immediately replace Vashti. Instead, he set off to invade Greece . . . and suffered a humiliating loss. When we turn to Esther 2:1 and read, "after these things," some years have passed. [11]

When we pick up the story, Xerxes had decided it was time to replace Vashti by hosting a beauty pageant of sorts. Instead of the glamorous contenders answering questions about world peace on live TV, however, one at a time these contestants were forced to spend the night with him. According to Esther 2:2, what were the prerequisites for becoming a "contestant"?

_____

(The historian Josephus estimates that 400 virgins were rounded up and taken to the harem.)[12]

According to verse 3, how would these women prepare for their night with the king?

_____

For how long would they prepare for their night with the king? _____ (v. 12)

What does verse 4 reveal about who would become queen?

_____

We tend to romanticize this passage, but in reality, this is an evil and degrading system that treated women as property.

Have you ever heard someone say that Christianity puts women down? Do you agree? Why or why not?

_____

_____

_____

It may be that some men wrongfully put women down, but how does the Bible teach a man to treat a woman? Look up 1 Timothy 5:1–2 and Ephesians 5:25–33 and record your answer:

_____

_____

_____

By contrast, the world often takes a dehumanizing view of women. Describe a commercial, ad, or magazine cover you saw recently that portrays how women are depicted in our culture.

_____

_____

_____

It seems that King Xerxes' view of women wasn't much different. In verse 14, we learn that after an evening with the king, where was the woman sent?

_____

_____

Essentially, they would become a prisoner in Xerxes' harem.

Where was God in all of this? And where is He today when men objectify women? Do you think God is absent or uncaring? Is any place too dark for God to be there? Explain your answer.

_____

_____

_____

_____

Write out Psalm 139:8–12.

_____

_____

_____

_____

God is always at work in every place, even in a pagan king's harem. While Esther was not rescued out of this oppressive system, in God's providence, she "gained favor" in the harem and before the king. God was working in Esther's circumstances to bring about judgment on the wicked as well as salvation for His people.

One day, our broken, fallen world will be done away with, and all things will be made new. And in the meantime, God is always attentive to His children, redeeming and bringing about His kingdom purposes—in His way and in His time.

Read Revelation 21:1–4. What promises from this passage are particularly meaningful to you and why? Write your thoughts below.

_____

_____

# Day 2: *Meet the Cast:*
## MORDECAI

*Read Esther 2:1–7.*

In Esther 2, we read that two of God's chosen people entered the secular arena of government. Everything about them stood in sharp contrast to what we have read about King Xerxes.

According to verse 5, Mordecai is identified as a _____ in Susa, from the tribe of

_____.

Based on verses 5–6, how had his relatives initially arrived?

_____

_____

Mordecai doesn't fit in; he belongs in Palestine. Read 1 Peter 2:11. Based on this verse, what do you have in common with Mordecai?

_____

_____

_____

Look up these two words from 1 Peter 2:11, and record their definitions.

S _____: _____

E _____: _____

Look up Philippians 3:20. According to this verse, as followers of Christ, where does our citizenship truly lie?

_____

_____

_____

Another way of stating this truth is: My true home is in _____.

How do these passages change your outlook on yourself and how you live today?

_____

_____

Esther 2:7 tells us Mordecai adopted his _____ after her dad and mom _____.

Tomorrow we'll learn more about this young woman. We'll also learn much more about Mordecai as this story unfolds—including how he comes to be hated by a man in power.

In spite of your status as an exile, God wants to use you to be a blessing to the world and to fulfill His kingdom purposes in it. Match each verse reference to the corresponding truth:

You are an ambassador for Christ.       John 17:18
Through you, God is making His appeal
to others, that they would be reconciled
to Him.

Jesus sent you into the world, just as the       2 Corinthians 5:20
Father sent Him into the world.

You are the light of the world.       Mark 16:15

Jesus has commissioned you to go into all       Matthew 5:14
the world and proclaim the gospel to the
whole creation.

From an earthly perspective, Mordecai was a nobody, powerless against the backdrop of a massive, totalitarian regime. But in the story God was writing, he played a significant role. Through his faithfulness and integrity, Mordecai was ultimately the key to foiling an evil plot against God's chosen people.

Do you ever feel like a nobody? If so, why?

_____

How do the verses in the chart above speak to the purpose God has for you?

_____

_____

# Day 3: *Meet the Cast:*
## ESTHER

*Read Esther 2:7–11.*

What do we learn about Esther from Esther 2:7?

_____

_____

What words or phrases does Scripture use to describe her in this verse? List them below.

_____

_____

_____

Her parents both died, so she was raised by her _____. Her young life was marked by tragedy … she was an orphan and exile. She was a young woman who had lots of reasons to not turn out well, but she turned into a beautiful, effective servant of the Lord.

What has the Lord overcome in your own life so He can use you for His purposes?

_____

_____

Esther is also _____ to look at. God gave her this beauty. It is part of His providence in her life.

We don't know whether Esther was taken voluntarily or against her will. But based on what we know about Xerxes, as well as the fact that verse 8 says that Esther was "_____ into the king's palace" and "put in _____," she was likely seized and held against her will.

Whether she went of her own free will or was coerced, Esther's story unfolds to reveal that we know God, in His providence, brought good out of evil.

What happens when Esther enters the palace (v. 9)?

_____

_____

As we continue reading chapter 2, we'll see that Esther wins the favor of others twice more. How does she do this? What makes her stand out?

_____

_____

_____

Where does favor ultimately come from? See Daniel 1:9 for the answer. (Daniel was also a prisoner in a king's palace!)

_____

_____

Ultimately, Esther and Daniel both gained favor because God had a plan to fulfill His redemptive purposes in this world through them.

Look up the following verses. Next to each one, write the name of the person who received the Lord's favor.

GENESIS 6:8 _____

GENESIS 39:4 _____

EXODUS 33:17 _____

1 SAMUEL 2:26 _____

LUKE 1:30 _____

Based on what you know about these stories, what do you think it means to have the Lord's "favor"?

_____

_____

As you read this story, you'll see that Esther was a woman of poise and admirable character.

In Esther 2:10, what does Mordecai command Esther not to do?

_____

_____

We'll learn later in the book that there were strong feelings of anti-Semitism in the highest places of government, so it was probably wise of Mordecai and Esther to not make her Jewish heritage public. What do you think it says about Esther's character that she continued to follow Mordecai's counsel, even after she'd left his direct care?

_____

_____

Esther may have felt abandoned and alone, separated from all that was familiar. But unbeknownst to her, she was being watched by someone who deeply cared for her.

According to verse 11, who was pacing back and forth in front of the harem's courtyard every day?

_____

_____

Why was he doing this?

_____

Mordecai's watchful care over his adopted daughter is a picture of God. When you are "imprisoned" in circumstances out of your control—even if you're to blame—you're not alone. You may feel trapped, with no way out, but your heavenly Father is there. The Lord watches what is happening to you and observes how you are doing. In time, God will defeat your enemy's objectives and fulfill His holy purpose for your life.

Write out Psalm 121:3–4, personalizing it with your own name.

_____

_____

_____

_____

_____

# Day 4: *True Beauty*

*Read Esther 2:12–17.*

What does Esther ask for when it's her turn to visit the king (2:15)?

_____

_____


First Timothy 6:6 says "godliness with contentment" is great _____.

Why is that (1 Timothy 6:7)?

_____

_____


What Esther-like woman do you know in your own life, and how does she demonstrate simplicity and contentment?

_____

_____

_____


Do you think that you too can become a woman who is content in any and every circumstance? Why or why not?

_____

_____

_____


Look up Philippians 4:11–13. Who learned contentment? _____ (See Phil. 1:1 if you need help.)

What is the "secret" to contentment (v. 13)?

_____

_____

Back to Esther ... she could have responded to this dramatic change of circumstances in one of two ways:

1. **By becoming demanding and controlling.** One day she's an orphan in a foreign land, and the next day she's a potential queen in the king's palace. This reversal in fortune could have gone to her head, but it didn't.

Are you tempted to become like the world around you? Or do you find it easy to remember, "I'm different"?

2. **In terror at the prospect of being taken into the king's chambers.** (Remember, Esther doesn't know how this story will end!)

We don't see her doing either. Instead, she illustrates the principles in 1 Peter 3:1–6. Read this passage, and then answer the following questions:

Where should our beauty *not* ultimately come from (v. 3)?

_____

_____

Where does true beauty come from (v. 4)?

_____

_____

How are we Sarah's daughters (v. 6)?

_____

_____

That's what we see in Esther. She likely experienced fear; but her actions show that she trusted that God's sovereignty was bigger than her fears. *Fear of God protected her from being paralyzed by fear of man.* This is beauty in the truest, purest sense of the word.

And King Xerxes took notice. What does Esther 2:16–17 say about his response to Esther?

_____

_____

_____

# Day 5: *A Plot Overturned*

*Read Esther 2:18–23.*

God had a plan to give us a Savior. What He did for Esther was a part of that plan.

Similarly, what happens in your life isn't disconnected from God's great, eternal plan. What is taking place in your life may have ramifications and implications centuries down the road.

What is the name of the feast King Xerxes throws in verse 18?

_____

What else does Xerxes do (v. 18)?

_____

Esther's life is already blessing the kingdom in ways she never could have anticipated. Her presence on the throne of Persia shows that God is going before His people to provide for their circumstances ahead of time.

God doesn't place Esther in the palace as an afterthought or as a knee-jerk reaction to Haman's cruel plot.

Read Deuteronomy 31:8. God is the God who sees what we need *beforehand* and provides.

What are you currently worried about?

_____

_____

Write out Psalm 139:5.

_____

_____

How does this verse provide hope in the face of the worries you recorded above?

_____

_____

God knows what will happen, and He has already gone before to provide for you. So don't stay up fretting, trying to figure it all out. God knows, cares, and has already provided for you!

*God, You know about _____. Help me to trust You with it.*

In Esther 2:21–23, we read a short account that seems unrelated to the details of this story. But in God's providence, years later, every detail will become important in salvation for His people. This is just another thread in the tapestry being woven by divine providence.

In verse 21, where is Mordecai sitting?

_____

_____

This is where commercial and legal business was transacted. It suggests that now Mordecai has risen to some position of responsibility in the city.

In verse 21, what news does Mordecai overhear?

_____

_____

God put Mordecai at the king's gate to hear this plot.

In spite of the fact that Xerxes is not a godly king, Mordecai is loyal to him. What does Mordecai do with the information (v. 22)?

_____

_____

These two men are tried and brought to justice, and the coup to overthrow King Xerxes is averted. In verse 23, where is this incident recorded?

_____

_____

However, Mordecai receives no official recognition, thanks, or reward for saving the king's life. Jump ahead to Esther 3:1. According to this verse, who is honored and advanced by the king?

_____

Mordecai's good deed went unrecognized—for now—while the man who would seek to destroy him was celebrated. This pattern is repeated often throughout history and at times in our own lives. Faithful people often go unrewarded, while evil people are sometimes exalted.

What is an area of your life where it's hard to see the benefits of faithfulness?

_____

What does God's Word teach will eventually happen, though?

_____ pursues sinners,

but the righteous are _____ with good (Prov. 13:21).

"The Son of Man is going to come with his angels in the glory of his Father, and then he will _____ each person according to what he has done" (Matt. 16:27).

What important reminder does Galatians 6:7 provide?

_____

_____

Faithfulness will be rewarded. Maybe not now—but ultimately. You will reap what you sow.

Based on past experiences, how do you think you would have responded if you had been overlooked as Mordecai was?

_____

_____

Look at this story and remember: God sees; God knows. He records your deeds in the history books of heaven, and He will reward you for faithfulness to Him in His time.

Circle back to your list of areas where it is hard to see the benefits of faithfulness. Next to each area, record the words "God sees" and "God knows" to remind yourself that your faithfulness does not ultimately go unrewarded.

Spend time meditating on and memorizing the following verse this week:

FOR WE DO NOT WRESTLE AGAINST FLESH AND BLOOD BUT...

AGAINST the spiritual forces of EVIL in the HEAVENLY PLACES.

EPHESIANS 6:12

# Week 3

## AN EVIL PLAN

If you could pick an emotion to describe the current status of our culture, what would it be? Anger would probably rank fairly high on the list. Everywhere we look, from social media to the news to drivers on the road, we find *someone* angry at *something*.

In our study this week, we'll look at how some of the main characters in the book of Esther reacted to the situation around them. There's Haman, who was angry about something he couldn't control, and then there's Esther and Mordecai, who chose to respond differently—in humility and brokenness. As we study these two contrasts, we'll be challenged to examine our own hearts and learn to trust the One who is in control of all circumstances.

## Day 1: The Trouble With Partial Obedience

*Read Esther 3.*

At the beginning of chapter 3, we're introduced to a new character: Haman the _____ (v. 1). This one word alone tells us plenty about Haman, so let's explore a brief history of this people.

Haman was a descendant of Agag, who was _____ (1 Sam. 15:8). The Amalekites were descendants of Esau (Gen. 36:12), Jacob's twin brother, and had been archenemies of the Jews for centuries.

*God Makes a Promise*

*Read Exodus 17:8–16.*

What people group was eager to attack the Israelites just after they escaped Egypt and crossed the Red Sea?

_____

At the end of that battle, God makes a significant promise to Moses. Read Exodus 17:14–16, and record God's promise here.

Moses builds an altar and says of God, "The Lord will have _____ with Amalek from generation to generation" (v. 16).

*A Failed Assignment*

Read 1 Samuel 15:2–9. What specific assignment does God give King Saul?

_____

_____

The time had come for the Amalekites to be destroyed. But Saul fails in his assignment. How (vv. 7–9)?

_____

_____

As a result of Saul's disobedience, not only did the Amalekites continue to exist for generations but they also persisted as a thorn in the side of the Jews.

God ordered the Amalekites to be destroyed while the Amalekites sought to destroy God's people. In Esther 3, we're introduced to another Agagite: Haman. His name will strike fear in the Jews as he uses his power to attempt to exterminate them.

Haman wouldn't even exist if centuries earlier Saul had obeyed in destroying God's enemies.

Pray, asking the Lord to reveal any areas of your life where you're "partially" obeying Him.

Have you considered how continuing in this sin could have implications for generations to come? Why or why not?

_____

_____

What step will you take today to turn from your sin and run to Christ?

_____

_____

# Day 2: *Meet the Cast:*
## HAMAN

*Read Esther 3:1–5.*

Yesterday we learned that Haman is an Agagite. Today we learn that he is growing in power. What position does King Xerxes give Haman in Esther 3:1?

_____

_____

What does the king command in verse 2?

_____

Who, however, refuses to bend his knee (v. 2)?

_____

Some believe Mordecai held a personal grudge against Haman, but it seems that his life was characterized by convictions, not pride.

How often did those around Mordecai try to change his mind (v. 4)?

_____

_____

No one could sway him, though. His life did not show evidence of being driven by fear of man but by fear of God.

To find out what your life is driven by, in the first column on the next page, record the areas in your life where you are living to please others. In the second column, record the areas in your life where you are living to please God.

| PLEASING OTHERS | PLEASING GOD |
| --- | --- |
| | |

Based on your response, what do you think drives you more—a desire to please others or a desire to please the Lord?

_____

_____

_____

What does God's Word have to say about this? Write out each of the following verses to find out.

PROVERBS 29:5 _____

_____

MATTHEW 10:28 _____

_____

HEBREWS 13:6 _____

_____

GALATIANS 1:10 _____

_____

Will you ask God to help you desire to please Him more and more? Write your prayer here:

_____

_____

_____

_____

When Haman realizes Mordecai will not bow to him, how does he respond (Est. 3:5)?

_____

_____

_____

Fury snarls, "I'll make you pay." And Haman has big plans for how to make Mordecai pay for this slight. Before we move on to those plans, we should pause and ask ourselves, "Is there any of Haman in me?"

What people or situations am I seeking to control?

_____

_____

How am I grasping for power?

_____

_____

_____

_____

When others don't do things my way, do I get bent out of shape?

_____

_____

_____

_____

# Day 3: *Under Attack*

*Read Esther 3:6–9.*

We've seen Haman's name before in the text. But what new description is added in Esther 3:10?

_____

_____

In verse 6, we learn that Haman is not content to simply make Mordecai pay. Who else does he want to destroy?

_____

_____

That sounds rather extreme to us, but remember that this battle is not ultimately between Haman and Mordecai. The same is true in your life. Who tends to *seem* like your enemy?

_____

_____

But who is your *actual* enemy, according to Ephesians 6:11–12?

_____

_____

_____

Haman and Mordecai are merely symbols of a collision, at a far deeper level, between God and Satan. (Although, don't forget—while God is eternal, Satan is a created being and his power is limited!)

How do we see this to be true in Job 2:1–6?

_____

_____

_____

The real battle in our world today is between Satan's temporal kingdom and God's eternal kingdom, and people are lining up on one side or the other. However, Satan is the loser in this battle. God will ultimately triumph.

Take some time to read about Satan's defeat recorded in Revelation 20:7–10. Write down any questions that you have about this passage in the space below.

_____

_____

_____

## Upstanding Citizens Under Attack

Once Haman conceives the plot, he goes to the king for backing and authority to implement it. According to verse 8, why does he tell the king he shouldn't tolerate these people?

_____

_____

In Jeremiah 29:7, we find that God commanded the Jews to be upstanding citizens. Fill in the blanks for the passage below to find out why.

"Seek the _____ of the city where I have sent you into _____, and _____ to the LORD on its behalf, for in its _____ you will find your _____."

Write out a list of specific ways you can start praying for your own community.

_____

_____

_____

Haman slanders the Jews to King Xerxes, though he doesn't specifically tell the king who these people are.

On what basis does Haman appeal to King Xerxes in Esther 3:9?

_____

_____

_____

Ten thousand talents of silver would be millions and millions of U.S. dollars in today's economy. Where would Haman come up with this money? He was likely planning to use the plunder from the Jews to pay back the king's treasury. Xerxes could have seen this offer as lucrative, since he'd recently been defeated by the Greeks. He likely sees the opportunity to recover some of his financial loss from that extensive battle.

We will see how the king responds to Haman's request in tomorrow's study. But to wrap up today, does it ever seem that Christians are under attack as "sojourners" and "exiles" (Remember 1 Peter 2:11)?

_____

_____

_____

_____

How does the Lord ask us to live in light of that reality through the following passages?

ROMANS 13:1-7 _____

_____

1 PETER 3:13-17 _____

_____

MATTHEW 22:17-22 _____

_____

1 THESSALONIANS 4:10-12 _____

_____

# Day 4: *A Study in Contrasts*

*Read Esther 3:10–11.*

What does the king give Haman in Esther 3:10?

_____

_____

_____

_____

This means Haman now has the authority to act in the king's name.

In this interaction, we see a casual disregard for human life, including that of the most defenseless: women and children, young and old. We saw it earlier in Xerxes' treatment of women and now in his quickness to issue a decree to exterminate an entire minority race.

This devaluing of life is characteristic of a perspective that doesn't recognize that God is the Creator and Giver of life. Where do you see life devalued in our own current culture?

_____

_____

_____

_____

_____

_____

How did Mordecai value the king's life in Esther 2?

_____

_____

_____

Esther and Mordecai are also concerned for the lives of their own people.

Let's pause the action for a minute to continue to contrast these two sets of characters: King Xerxes and his prime minister, Haman, and Mordecai and his cousin Esther. As you're comparing the two, circle the characteristics that describe you.

| KING XERXES AND HAMAN | MORDECAI AND ESTHER |
|---|---|
| Wealthy, powerful, influential | Poor, with no influence . . . or so they think |
| Insecure about losing their prestige and position | Nothing to lose, therefore nothing to fear |
| Driven to control others | Willing to be under God's control |
| Arrogant and proud | Humble and meek |
| Not self-controlled | Self-controlled |
| Influenced by the opinions of others | Driven by principle |
| Protective of reputation and image | Protective of others |
| Self-centered | Others-centered |
| Centered their worlds around themselves | Aligned themselves with God's plan |
| Insulated themselves from the plight of others | Identified with the plight of others |
| Used their position to serve themselves | Used their position to serve others |
| Controlling of others | Sought to serve others |
| Impetuous | Restrained |
| Emotionally unstable | Emotionally stable |
| Exalted themselves, therefore God humbled them | Humbled themselves, therefore God exalted them |

Which set of people do you most resemble?

_____

_____

As "new creatures" in Christ, we are to "put off" anything and everything that is a part of our old, corrupt flesh—sinful habits, wrong attitudes, impure motives, and so on. But it's not enough just to "put off" the old life. In its place, by God's grace and by the power of His Holy Spirit, we must actively "put on the new self"—qualities of the life of Christ within us.

Read Ephesians 4:17–32. Fill in the columns below.

| PUT OFF . . . | PUT ON . . . |
| --- | --- |
|  |  |

When you are finished, spend time alone with God in confession and prayer, using this list as a guide. In the days ahead, take time to read and meditate on the Scripture verses that relate to the items you have listed, and ask the Lord to help you "put on" the characteristics that bear His image.

## Day 5: *Hope Is Not Lost*

*Read Esther 3:12–15.*

We're all thrilled to receive an old-fashioned letter in the mail (just as long as it's not another bill to pay). But today, you'll see the Jews receiving a letter that contains news infinitely worse than any bill.

According to what you've just read, what instructions do these letters include?

_____

_____

This edict seems so final. There seems to be no escape.

What news have you received that seems final and hopeless?

_____

_____

_____

_____

**But God.** God is the King over all the earth. No edict can force His hand. God, in His sovereignty, is using people to fulfill His purposes and bring about His kingdom on this earth, even now. Even when everything around us seems to indicate otherwise.

The text doesn't spell out exactly what God was doing at this moment in history, but we do know what He was *not doing*:

He was *not* sitting in heaven wringing His hands.

He was *not* surprised or thrown off course by the king's edict.

He was *not* scrambling to come up with a way to save His people.

God not only knew this was going to happen, He had already gone before. What's the word for that?

_____

He had set in motion a plan to thwart Haman's wicked intentions, long before Haman acted in hatred toward the Jews. He had positioned one of His servants, Mordecai, at the king's gate, and He had positioned another of His servants, Esther, on the queen's throne.

What evil has surfaced in your world, workplace, home, church, or school?

_____

_____

_____

Remember that God has already readied the instruments to overrule that evil in His way and in His time.

As you look at your own life circumstances, prayerfully consider, "For what purpose may God have placed me here at this time"? Write down any ideas that come to mind.

_____

_____

_____

_____

_____

_____

Spend time meditating on and memorizing the following verse this week:

"WHO KNOWS WHETHER YOU HAVE NOT
COME TO THE KINGDOM

## for such a time as this?"

ESTHER 4:14

# Week 4

## FOR SUCH A TIME AS THIS

Have you ever been in the right place at the right time? Maybe it was to offer aid to someone in distress, make a contact that got you the job you'd been dreaming of, or help diffuse a tense situation that could have escalated out of control.

This week, we come to the most famous verse in the book of Esther: "For such a time as this." God placed Esther in the right place at the right time, not only to save the Jewish people but to display His glory. And just like Esther, God has placed us in our homes, our jobs, our culture, and in this time of history on purpose for a purpose. As you study God's Word this week, may your eyes be opened to His purpose for you, in "such a time as this," so that you may help to further His kingdom.

## Day 1: *Sackcloth and Ashes*

*Read Esther 4–5.*

In Esther 4:1–2, we see Mordecai grieving over the king's edict. What does Mordecai do? Circle all that apply:

- Stays home in bed for days.

- Tears his clothes.

- Goes to the king to appeal for His people.

- Numbs his pain with alcohol or another substance.

- Spirals downward in depression.

- Cries out loudly and bitterly in the middle of the city.

- Dresses in sackcloth and ashes.

This expression of grief may seem extreme to us, but Mordecai has nothing to lose. There's nowhere left for him to turn but to God. So he doesn't hold back; he unapologetically makes a scene in public.

Have you ever made a scene in public out of distress or felt like doing so? What was the cause?

_____

_____

_____

In the midst of difficult circumstances, it's hard to see what God has planned.

*Sackcloth and Ashes*

Mordecai clothed himself in sackcloth. Sackcloth was a coarse material, usually made of black goat's hair, so it was quite uncomfortable to wear. Putting it on was an outward sign of a person's inward condition of humility, contrition, brokenness, and mourning.[15]

In Scripture, we see people putting on sackcloth and ashes for different reasons. Look up the following verses, and write the reason people donned sackcloth and ashes:

GENESIS 37:34


JONAH 3:5


These are snapshots of individuals and cultures who clearly took their sin seriously.

Do we live in a culture that takes sin seriously or casually? How can you tell?

_____

_____

While you probably don't have any sackcloth in your closet, what would it look like for you to dress in humility, contrition, brokenness, and mourning over your sin?

_____

_____

Look up the following verses. What humble step does each one encourage us to take?

LUKE 18:9-14

JAMES 5:16

PROVERBS 12:1

EPHESIANS 4:32

Mordecai wasn't the only one who mourned over this edict. According to Esther 4:3, who else did?

_____

_____

When is the last time you mourned, wept, and fasted?

_____

_____

_____

Why wait until the next big crisis to call out to God? Do so now. Humble yourself. Cry out to Him. Take some time today to meditate on Psalm 51 and ask God to create a clean heart within you.

## Day 2: *Is Your Head in the Sand?*

*Read Esther 4:1–12.*

What news caused Esther deep distress (v. 4)?

_____

_____

This means Esther writhed in vehement pain. [16] Perhaps her stomach hurt or her hands became clammy. She knew something was wrong, and she was disturbed.

Can you think of a time when bad news caused you to be in physical pain?

_____

_____

_____

Read Luke 22:39–44. What caused Jesus to be in "agony"?

_____

_____

_____

Back to Esther. According to verses 4–5, how did she first try to help?

_____

_____

_____

When Mordecai wouldn't accept her gift, what did Esther do?

_____

_____

Esther cared enough about Mordecai to investigate what was happening.

## Understanding the Times

Do you know what's going on in the world and how it's affecting the people of God? Or are you sticking your head in the sand, oblivious to what's happening around you? Are you content to stay in your Christian bubble as long as you're safe and unaffected? Using the scale, rate how knowledgeable you are of the times in which you're living.

HEAD'S BURIED          SOMEWHERE IN THE MIDDLE          DON'T MISS A THING

1        2        3        4        5        6        7        8        9        1 0

What does Hebrews 13:3 say we ought to do about this?

_____

_____

Are you educated about your brothers and sisters around the world who are being persecuted for their faith? (Read the sidebar at the beginning of this week's study to get started.)

_____

_____

## Within the Church

There's something else you need to be aware of that's even more subtle. The main problem isn't what's happening *to* the people of God but what's happening *in* the people of God. We can't expect the world to be godly. It doesn't know God. The worldliness of the Church should cause us just as much distress.

How does the Church look just like the world? How does it look different?

_____

_____

Esther's response should also be ours: "I'm willing to leave the comfort, security, and convenience I know in order to do something about what's going on among the people of God, even if it costs my life."

How can you specifically grow in your knowledge of what is happening to and in the Church? What can you do to help?

_____

_____

## The Stakes Are High

In Esther 4:6–9, Mordecai sends instructions for Esther to plead with the king on behalf of her people. Esther has been accustomed to obeying Mordecai, but the stakes are extremely high this time.

According to verse 11, how many days had passed since Esther had been called to come to the king?

_____

_____

What does this verse tell us the law stated about approaching the king uninvited?

_____

_____

Obeying Mordecai may cost Esther her life. It seems she has two choices.

CHOICE 1: She can depend on her position within the palace, hoping to save her own skin and refusing to violate the king's law.

CHOICE 2: She can risk everything for the chance to save the lives of her people.

Ultimately, we know that Esther chose not to play it safe and that her people were spared. But imagine if she had made choice #1. Knowing what you know about the sovereignty and providence of God, how do you predict this story would have ended differently?

_____

_____

_____

Take time now to pray for Christian brothers and sisters facing persecution around the globe. For up-to-date information, check out The Voice of the Martyrs. You can receive weekly prayer requests from them at ICommitToPray.com.

## Day 3: For Such a Time as This

*Read Esther 4:13–15.*

In verse 13, Mordecai doesn't pull any punches. He begins by reminding Esther that she too is a _____. If her people perish, she will perish, too. Her life is at risk whether she does or doesn't go into the king.

Mordecai goes on to confidently assert that if Esther doesn't speak up, God will still rescue them. Fill in the blank for his words recorded in verse 14: "Relief and deliverance will rise for the Jews from _____."

How can he be so sure?

This is an expression of faith. Mordecai knows God will not forget His covenant with Abraham. God will not allow His people to be wiped out. What promise(s) of God are you confident of and clinging to, even in the midst of frightening circumstances? Write them below.

_____

_____

_____

If you're not sure, look up the following promises recorded in Scripture. Put a check mark next to any you choose to hold tightly to.

___ God's love will never fail (1 Chron. 16:34).

___ All things will work out for the good of God's children (Rom. 8:28).

___ God will comfort us in our trials (2 Cor. 1:3–4).

___ God will finish the work He started in you (Phil. 1:6).

___ Christ will return for us (John 14:2–3).

Mordecai is reminding Esther that while God might use her to accomplish His purposes, God doesn't ultimately *need* her. He will provide whether she is obedient or not. The same is true for us. Amazingly, God often chooses to work through us. However, we're not indispensable. God will accomplish His purposes with or without us.

## For Such a Time As This

Mordecai then asks Esther, "Who knows whether you have not come to the kingdom for such a time as this?" (v. 14). Mordecai is saying this is the equation:

*you + this position + this time = God's providence*

All the blessings you enjoy aren't ultimately for your happiness. The home you were born into, the opportunities you've had, the culture and era you live in—all of these things exist according to God's providence and for His purposes.

Look up Acts 17:26–27, and fill in the blanks:

> [God] made from one man every nation of mankind to live on all the
> face of the earth, having determined _____ and the boundaries
> of their _____, that they should _____,
> and perhaps feel their way toward him and find him. Yet he is actually not
> far from each one of us.

You are not in the position you are in by accident. God has a job with your name on it. You may think, *I don't have a position of great influence. It's all I can do to survive. I'm just trying to keep my head above water.*

Look beyond the boundaries of *your* kingdom. God has put you here, for such a time as this, with an incredible opportunity to represent Him and *His* kingdom.

It's not by chance that you are where you are today at this time and place. As you think about your life and the providence of God, write down what God has entrusted to you to further His kingdom here on earth:

ABILITIES:

EXPERIENCES:

INFLUENCE:

RELATIONSHIPS:

MATERIAL RESOURCES:

How are you stewarding, or how can you better steward, these gifts for God's glory and for such a time as this?

_____

_____

_____

# Day 4: *A Time to Act*

*Read Esther 4:16–5:2.*

In today's passage, Esther decided to get involved. According to verse 16, what did she decide needed to happen first?

_____

_____

_____

In essence, Esther resolved, "I'm going to the king, after we go to the King." The text doesn't explicitly state that prayer was involved, but we can assume God's people were praying. They didn't skip meals just to feel hungry but to express their desperation to see God intervene. This was a situation they couldn't solve through ordinary means.

Is there a situation in your life that needs to be confronted?

_____

_____

_____

Before you dive into a difficult problem, humble yourself. Seek God's direction through prayer.

Possibly even fast and get others to seek God with you as Esther did. Fasting is a sign of humbling ourselves and acknowledging our need for God.

## Surrendering to the King of Kings

Is Esther is being melodramatic in verse 16 when she says, "If I _____, I _____"?

Why or why not? _____

Remember it's *the law* that the moment she steps across the threshold into Xerxes' throne room—except in the unlikely event that he holds out his golden scepter—she receives an automatic sentence of death.

Remember also the kind of man this king is. History has shown him to be hot-tempered and impetuous. Based on his treatment of Vashti, he may be the kind of guy who acts and then thinks. His temperament could cost Esther her life.

In spite of all this, Esther has come to the point of total abandon and surrender to God's purposes.

Look up Luke 9:23. According to Jesus, how often must we choose to surrender to His will for our lives?

_____

_____

What does this look like practically in your life?

_____

_____

_____

According to Esther 5:1, how does Esther prepare to face the king? Why do you think she does this?

_____

_____

Imagine the shocked silence that descends on the throne room as Esther dares to step into that room. Perhaps everyone was holding their breath, wondering, *What will the king do?* Verse 2 tells us. What happens when the king sees Queen Esther standing in the court?

_____

_____

_____

Whew! Esther must have sighed in relief.

Read Revelation 19:16. What names are given to Jesus in this passage? What King had ultimate authority over King Xerxes?

_____

_____

_____

King Xerxes was powerful, but he was not outside of God's control. That's true of the worst tyrants in history. It was true of Adolf Hitler, Saddam Hussein, and Fidel Castro, and it's true of the mini-tyrants who may be a part of your life.

Remind yourself of the truth from Proverbs 21:1 you memorized during week one. Rewrite this passage with the name of any people or circumstances that seem to be ruling over you.

_____ heart is a stream of water in the hand of the LORD;
he turns it wherever he will.

## Day 5: *Esther's Restraint vs. Haman's Roller Coaster*

*Read Esther 5:3–9.*

What does Esther request of the king in verse 4?

_____

Why do you think Esther didn't simply ask Xerxes outright to save her people?

_____

_____

At the feast, the king again asks Esther about her wish. What is Esther's response in verses 5–8?

_____

_____

Movement is occuring on two levels. On the divine level, God is restraining Esther from speaking what's on her mind, because He is still working behind the scenes. On a human level, Esther seems to realize it's not yet the right time. Her restraint, patience, and wisdom is truly amazing.

She knows the king loves banquets. Can you remember how long the feast recorded in Esther 1 was? (Hint: look on page 12.) She behaves in ways that are sensitive to others and to the Lord, allowing God to create the circumstances that would prove to be Haman's undoing rather than forcing it herself.

Review the following verses:

ESTHER 2:16–18

ESTHER 5:2–3

ESTHER 5:4–5

What words would you use to describe the way the king responds to Esther in these interactions?

_____

_____

_____

Based on what you know of Esther's character, why do you think she didn't make outright demands of the king?

_____

_____

_____

_____

When is the last time you marched right in to someone and said something you thought needed to be said? How did it go? Did you regret it later? Why or why not?

_____

_____

_____

According to verse 9, how did Haman leave the feast?

_____

_____

In the same verse, we see a dramatic change of temperature in Haman's countenance and spirit.

What emotion replaced his gladness?

_____

_____

_____

What caused this change?

_____

_____

In contrast to Esther's extraordinary self-control, Haman's emotions swing wildly. His sense of wellbeing seems dependent on external circumstances. When Esther favors him, his spirit soars. When Mordecai refuses to honor him, he sinks into depression.

How about you? Are you easily elated? Easily deflated?

_____

_____

_____

Pause and ask God to give you faith and joy in the truth that He is orchestrating every moment of your life.

Spend time meditating on and memorizing the following verse this week:

WHOEVER EXALTS HIMSELF WILL BE

# HUMBLED,

AND WHOEVER HUMBLES HIMSELF WILL BE

# EXALTED

MATTHEW 23:12

# Week 5

If you've ever seen the back of an embroidered design, it's a mess. There's threads of different colors that don't resemble any clear picture at all. But when you turn it over to see the front … only then does the overall design become clear.

Our lives may sometimes look like the back of that embroidery—all tangled and messed up. We can't see any purpose in it. But, as we learn from Esther and Mordecai's example this week, we have to trust that the Lord is orchestrating our lives and causing all things to work together for good, even if we can't see it in that moment. If your life feels messy this week, consider the verses in this week's study to be an invitation to flip the picture over and see the beautiful handiwork of God.

## God Moves in a Mysterious Way
### by William Cowper

God moves in a mysterious way
His wonders to perform;
He plants His footsteps in the sea
And rides upon the storm.

Deep in unfathomable mines
Of never failing skill
He treasures up His bright designs
And works His sov'reign will.

Ye fearful saints, fresh courage take;
The clouds ye so much dread
Are big with mercy and shall break
In blessings on your head.

Judge not the Lord by feeble sense,
But trust Him for His grace;
Behind a frowning providence
He hides a smiling face.

His purposes will ripen fast,
Unfolding every hour;
The bud may have a bitter taste,
But sweet will be the flow'r.

Blind unbelief is sure to err
And scan His work in vain;
God is His own interpreter,
And He will make it plain.

# Day 1: *Bitter Misery, Providential Hope*

*Read Esther 6.*

Review Esther 5:10–12. What does Haman boast of? Circle all that apply.

GOOD LOOKS

FAMILY

WEALTH

A FAST CAR

ACCOMPLISHMENTS

HONORS

EXALTATION

SCHOOLING

THE QUEEN'S INVITATION

As Haman is making his "I'm a V.I.P." speech to his family and friends, picture his jaw locking up and his face tightening. According to verse 13, why can't he enjoy his moment of fame?

_____

_____

_____

In spite of all his wealth, prestige, and influence, Haman is rendered miserable by the sight of one little "nobody" whom he can't control.

Isn't it interesting how often the object of our bitterness begins to control us? Can you relate? Do you find you can't enjoy God's blessings because you're consumed with how that person hurt you?

_____

_____

_____

_____

What simple solution do Haman's wife and friends offer in verse 14?

_____

_____

_____

Does Haman listen?

_____

_____

_____

The gallows were seventy-five feet high or about eight stories tall. We're not sure if the structure was actually that high or if it was placed on a hill or a building that made it that high. At any rate, it could probably be seen all across the city.

Why do you think Haman ordered the gallows to be built to such extreme specifications?

_____

_____

## When Things Go from Bad to Worse

Esther, Mordecai, and the Jews prayed and fasted, but it didn't seem to be working. Things were getting worse, not better. Haman's hatred led him to build gallows to hang Mordecai on the next day.

What situation in your life seems to be growing worse in spite of your prayers?

_____

_____

_____

Don't panic, and don't be afraid to act when it's time to act. Instead, through it all, trust God with the results, even when circumstances appear to indicate your destruction. God is still in control, providentially ordering all things to fulfill His purposes.

What in life doesn't make sense to you?

_____

_____

Know that it makes perfect sense to God. God often picks the time that looks the darkest and the most hopeless to show His power and glory. Why? Perhaps, so no human can take the credit. His grace always shines against the darkest backdrop.

To remind yourself of this truth, read through the scenes of the crucifixion recorded in Matthew 27. This moment must have seemed incredibly dark. Yet what was God doing?

_____

_____

# Day 2: One Eventful Night

_Read Esther 6:1–5._

Esther 6:1 opens with, "On that night …" What night is it exactly?

* It's the night Esther hosted her first feast for the king and Haman.
* It's the night Haman went home to his wife and vented his hatred for Mordecai.
* It's the night Haman ordered extravagant gallows to be built for Mordecai's hanging.

According to verse 1, who was having insomnia the same night all of this happened?

_____

A sleepless night wouldn't be worth mentioning in most books, let alone the Bible—unless God was orchestrating the king's sleeplessness in order to accomplish His purposes.

What reading does the king request when he realizes he isn't falling asleep?

_____

According to verse 2, out of all the king's chronicles, which story "just happens" to be read to the king?

_____

_____

What are the chances of this story being read? Is this a coincidence? No way! God providentially delayed Mordecai's reward for his good deed until the precise moment when the Jews needed supernatural deliverance.

That's something Mordecai could have been bitter over. After all, he had revealed a plot to attack and harm the king. (Revisit Esther 2:21–23 if you need a refresher.) But as we explored before, Mordecai's words and behavior showed no signs of bitterness.

Is there anything you're still bitter over? Write down anything that comes to mind.

_____

_____

_____

What does Ephesians 4:31 ask us to do with bitterness?

_____

_____

_____

Why is this step often challenging?

_____

_____

_____

How would truly understanding and resting in God's providence free you to release your bitterness?

_____

_____

_____

When Xerxes learned that Mordecai was not honored for his service, he asked who was in the court. Read verse 4. Who *just* arrived and for what purpose?

_____

_____

This feels like a well-scripted Hollywood movie scene. But it isn't. This is the true story of the split-second timing of God. What if Haman had arrived an hour later? The king would have found somebody else in the court to help honor Mordecai.

Can you think of a time in your life when you witnessed the split-second timing of God? Write about it below.

_____

_____

_____

_____

Perhaps Haman had been waiting for dawn all night so he could come to the king's palace and say, "Let's hang Mordecai." But before he could get the words out of his mouth, in God's precise timing, the king asked Haman what could be done to honor Mordecai.

Here we see that God is in charge of seemingly insignificant decisions and schedules. There are no chance happenings in this world! How does this encourage your heart today?

_____

_____

_____

# Day 3: *The Problem with Pride*

*Read Esther 6:6–14.*

In his pride, who does Haman assume the king wants to honor (v. 6)?

_____

_____

Can you think of a time when your pride caused you to act foolishly?

_____

_____

What does Haman recommend the king do for the man he wants to honor (vv. 7–9)?

1.

2.

3.

4.

What do you think Haman's suggestion, that he should be honored by wearing the king's robes and riding the king's horse, reveals about his heart?

_____

_____

Read verses 10–11. Put yourself in Haman's shoes. What do you imagine this moment is like for him?

_____

_____

This is God's providence at work! Fill in the blanks for Matthew 23:12:

"Whoever _____ himself will be _____, and whoever _____ himself will be _____."

How have you seen this to be true in your life?

_____

_____

Think back to the examples of bitterness you wrote about yesterday. Are any of them rooted in feelings of being underappreciated or undervalued?

_____

_____

Everything you have done for the glory of God will one day be rewarded. Humble yourself by surrendering your expectations for recognition or acclaim. God will exalt you in due time. Let Him choose when and how the reward will come.

Read Proverbs 18:12, and write down what individuals from the book of Esther these phrases describe:

"Before destruction a man's heart is haughty." _____

"Humility comes before honor." _____

In Haman's blind self-absorption, he actually sets in motion the circumstances that will lead to his own destruction and Mordecai's exaltation.

What does Esther 6:12 say each man did next?

MORDECAI: _____

HAMAN: _____

There's no evidence that Mordecai gloats over what just happened. He simply returns to what he had been doing—serving the king.

Haman, however, acted embarrassed and ashamed. The citizens of Susa likely knew Haman hated Mordecai. Mordecai's public recognition meant Haman's public humiliation. Everything went exactly the opposite of how Haman intended it to go.

## A Victim Mentality

In verse 13, what does Haman tell his wife and friends?

_____

_____

_____

Does he take responsibility for his troubles?

_____

_____

_____

Where does his focus seem to be?

_____

_____

_____

Rather than encouraging Haman to humble himself, take responsibility, and repent, his wife and friends took on a fatalistic attitude and told him what in verse 13?

_____

_____

_____

Then, in verse 14, Haman was whisked away to the second feast Esther has prepared for him and the king. Buckle up; this will prove to be one drama-filled feast!

Sometimes the hard things in our lives are the consequences of our own choices. Take a minute to ask, "Could these negative things I'm experiencing possibly be consequences of my pride, foolishness, or wrong choices?"

_____

_____

_____

# Day 4: *Esther's Appeal*

*Read Esther 7:1–5.*

I'm sure you've heard the old saying, "Silence is golden." Esther's story proves this is not always true.

## A Time to Speak

Ecclesiastes 3:1, 7 tells us, "For everything there is a _____, and a time for every matter under heaven . . . a time to keep _____, and a time to _____."

In Esther 2:10, Mordecai told Esther to _____. But in Esther 4:14, what did Mordecai tell Esther it was time to do? _____

Read James 1:19. What general guideline does Scripture give us about when to speak up?

_____

_____

When is a time you kept quiet when you should have spoken up or spoke up when you should have remained silent?

_____

_____

*Learning from Esther's Appeal*

What does the king ask Esther in Esther 7:2? Write down his words.

_____

_____

_____

This was the third time the king asked Esther what she wanted. If Esther had immediately shared her request, things may not have turned out as they did. She couldn't have known exactly what God was orchestrating, yet we see her wisely waiting. Finally, it was time for her to speak.

Read verses 3–4, and then answer these questions:

What words showcase Esther's humility and respect for her husband?

_____

What specific request does she make?

_____

How does the king respond in verse 5?

_____

How does Esther answer?

_____

With this interaction in mind, here are a few questions to ask yourself before you seek to wisely appeal to authority:

What is my specific request?

_____

Is my appeal humble or proud?

_____

Is my appeal respectful or accusatory?

_____

Is my appeal in my authority's best interest?

_____

# Day 5: _Finally Exposed_

_Read Esther 7:6–10._

Esther finally exposed Haman for who he really was. According to verse 6, what did Haman feel in response to Esther's words?

_____

_____

According to verse 7, what emotion does King Xerxes feel?

_____

_____

In a split second, Haman seemed to realize the party was over. Haman's demise represents the way things always end with the wicked.

Read Psalm 7:14–16, and record in column two how you see these truths at play in the book of Esther.

Behold, the wicked man conceives evil

and is pregnant with mischief

and gives birth to lies.

He makes a pit, digging it out,

and falls into the hole that he has made.

His mischief returns upon his own head,

and on his own skull his violence
descends.

In Esther 7:8, the king "just happens" to return to the room as Haman is doing what?

_____

_____

Again, we see God's providence at work through His split-second timing and divine orchestration.

The scene provides the motivation Xerxes needs to sign the death penalty for Haman. Ironically, how does Xerxes determine to kill Haman (vv. 9–10)?

_____

Haman's story is a picture of the truth that every enemy of God and His people will ultimately be destroyed.

Sometimes when we look at things as they are now, we feel the gravitational pull of despair. Esther's story reminds us that the way things are now is not the way they will always be.

What powerful truth do these passages teach? Write your responses below.

1 SAMUEL 2:10 _____

_____

_____

PSALM 75:10 _____

_____

_____

PSALM 145:20 _____

_____

_____

Spend time meditating on and memorizing the following verse this week:

YOU HAVE TURNED FOR ME MY
*MOURNING* INTO
*dancing:*
YOU HAVE LOOSED
MY SACKCLOTH AND
CLOTHED
ME WITH
*gladness*

PSALM 30:11

# Week 6

When you began this study, what did you think the book of Esther was mainly about? For a lot of us, we immediately thought about the courage of a queen. But hopefully as you've dug into God's Word, you've found that Esther also teaches us about practical issues like anger, pride, selfishness—and throughout points us to the sovereignty and providence of God in our lives.

As you head into the final stretch of our study, may you find renewed hope that God is working in the circumstances of your life today. He has not forgotten you; He knows your story and is writing the script for your life. Your story is really God's story.

## Purim in the 21st Century

Over 2,500 years later, the Jewish people still celebrate Purim each year. On the day before Purim, Jews fast from dawn to dusk as a reminder of Esther's call to fast due to Haman's decree to obliterate the Jews. That evening, the Jews go to the synagogue to read the book of Esther aloud.

Every time the name Haman is read (fifty-three times), the audience boos, hisses, and shouts, "May his name be blotted out!" Children blow horns and shake rattles, trying to drown out his name. It's a very dramatic celebration of the account of Esther.

Then, on the next day (the thirteenth day of the twelfth month of the Jewish Calendar, which usually coincides with March), Jews go back to the synagogue to read the book of Esther once more. They then celebrate at home with a holiday meal full of special foods, as well as a gift exchange. They also send food and gifts to the poor, much as it's described in the book of Esther.[17]

# Day 1: Let Us Then Draw Near

*Read Esther 8.*

What a difference one day can make! Read Esther 8:1–2, and record how are the tables are turned.

_____

_____

Haman was hanged on the gallows he constructed for Mordecai. Mordecai replaced Haman as the prime minister of the largest kingdom in the world. Everything has been turned upside down, inside out. While we can read the entirety of this story in Esther, we can't read the last chapter of our life stories. Everything can change in a moment. God is still on His throne, and with Him, *nothing* is impossible!

Read Psalm 37 and record a couple of truths that would have encouraged Esther and Mordecai had they read them in the middle of their circumstances. Then, write what verses or truths encourage you today.

_____

_____

_____

_____

Jumping to Revelation 11:15, how does Mordecai's story picture what will happen in the future?

_____

_____

_____

Back to the book of Esther . . . Haman was brought to justice and Mordecai was exalted, but in the first verses of chapter 8, the dreaded edict was still in effect. The Persians were still planning to annihilate the Jews.

So Esther implored the king again.

Read Esther 8:3–6. Write a summary of Esther's request in your own words.

_____

_____

Esther's request teaches us much about intercessory prayer. As you read verses 3–6, write the verse number next to each bullet point that describes what is happening in that verse.

- Esther is persistent (v. ___).
- Esther is earnest (v. ___).
- Esther makes a righteous request (v. ___).
- Esther is humble and submissive; not demanding (v. ___).
- Esther makes a specific request (v. ___).
- Esther personally identifies with her people (v. ___).

In verse 4, the king again granted Esther access to himself. A wonderful thing about the gospel is that in Christ we have been granted access to the throne room of God!
How are believers invited to approach God's throne in Hebrews 4:16?

_____

_____

We see the king's response to Esther in Esther 8:7–8. Unfortunately, his hands were tied, as the original edict spelling out the doom of the Jews was irrevocable. So what does he do?

_____

_____

Take some time now to practice intercessory prayer. Identify someone in your life who needs the Lord's help, and pray through the steps we learned from Esther in the bulleted list above.

## Day 2 : *Victory Day!*

*Read Esther 8:15–17.*

On May 7, 1945, Germany officially surrendered to the Allies, and the next day was declared "Victory in Europe Day." That announcement set off wild celebrations all around the world, with singing, dancing, and partying in the streets.[18]

The war wasn't yet over in the Pacific. Japan didn't surrender for another three months, but people knew that victory was at hand. Word traveled quickly, and celebrations broke out. That's a picture of what we see in Esther 8.

The old edict to annihilate the Jews couldn't be revoked, but the king gave Mordecai permission to issue a new edict saying the Jews could defend themselves. Though the battle hadn't happened, God's people were thrilled. They knew there was *hope*.

According to verse 15, after Mordecai was in the presence of the king, what did he emerge wearing?

_____

_____

What a contrast this is to how he was dressed at the beginning of chapter 4! Do you remember what he was wearing then?

_____

How did the city respond to Mordecai?

_____

_____

Review Esther 3:15. How has the atmosphere in the city changed?

_____

_____

Describe or draw a picture of the celebration described in Esther 8:16–17.

It was Victory Day! The war still needed to be fought, but now the people had hope. This was true not only of the Jews in Esther; it's true of us, God's people.

## Christ, Our Deliverer

Christ is your Deliverer! He has written, signed, and sealed an edict that says you can have victory over the law of sin and death. He has issued a decree that spells your freedom.

The apostle Paul describes this battle against the law of sin and death in Romans 7:18–21. Write out this passage below.

_____

_____

_____

_____

Paul goes on to say this in verses 22–24:

> For I delight in the law of God, in my inner being, but I see in my members another law waging war against the law of my mind and making me captive to the law of sin that dwells in my members. Wretched man that I am! Who will deliver me from this body of death?

Go back through the passage and circle the word "law."

What two laws is Paul contrasting in Romans 7?

_____

_____

That old law—the law of sin—is binding. But praise God! That old edict has been overcome by a higher, more powerful law. Through the death and resurrection of Christ, God put another law into effect.

What is the new edict?

_____

Look up James 1:25. How does this verse describe the law?

_____

_____

We are under an edict of freedom. Christ secured our freedom from sin and death through His sacrifice on the cross.

*Cause for Celebration*

Paul points to it in Romans 7:24–25: "Who will deliver me from this body of _____? Thanks be to _____ through _____!"

Mordecai was in the palace. Christ is seated at the right hand of the Father. He has been exalted, and He is your hope. He has issued a new edict that gives you the ability to overcome the law of sin.

Paul goes on to say in Romans 8:1, "There is therefore now no _____ for those who are _____."

Yes, that old edict is in effect, but no, it doesn't have to rule your life. Why? Write out the answer found in Romans 8:2.

_____

_____

Journal a prayer to God now, asking Him to open your eyes to just how much you have to celebrate in Christ.

_____

_____

# Day 3: *The Battle*

*Read Esther 9:1–16.*

In Esther 9, we finally read about the day the Jews must have dreaded for months: the thirteenth day of the month of Adar.

Review Esther 3:12–15. What command and edict were to be carried out on this day? Instead, what happened?

_____

_____

Once again, we see the split-second timing of God. The Jews were a small minority; this was a miraculous intervention on their behalf proving God fights for His people.

In Esther 9:2, the Jews gathered to defend themselves, and "no one could stand against them." Why?

_____

_____

_____

_____

According to verses 2–4, who came to the Jews' aid and why?

_____

_____

Mordecai had feared no one but God, but now others were afraid of him.

Was this a defensive or an aggressive war on the Jews' part? Read verses 5, 6, and 10 for clues.

_____

_____

Verse 6 says the Jews killed 500 men in Susa, and then the author takes the time to list the names of ten other men who were killed. Why do you think the author of this book highlights these names (v. 10).

_____

_____

_____

In verse 13, what does Esther ask of the king?

_____

_____

What phrase do you see repeated in verses 10, 15, and 16?

_____

_____

Read 1 Samuel 15. What did God instruct Saul to do with the plunder from the Amalekites?

_____

_____

Based on this passage, how did Saul respond to this instruction (circle one)?

FULLY  *or*  PARTIALLY

The Jews in Esther's day were acting out of self-defense. Unlike Saul, they weren't trying to get rich off their enemies.

## Take Up Arms

Being a warrior is part of the Christian life. This doesn't mean we act warlike or attack those who don't agree with us. But we do resist our sinful flesh, Satan, and this world system that has set itself against God.

We battle now, knowing that the day is coming when Christ's triumph will be complete over all His enemies.

You have enemies to battle too. Who are they?

1 JOHN 2:15 _____

GALATIANS 5:17 _____

1 PETER 5:8-9 _____

How are you doing in your daily battle against all three?

_____

_____

_____

_____

# Day 4: *Celebrate!*

*Read Esther 9:17–32.*

Great plots in literature have tension and then relief. Today is the big sigh of relief in this story. There's been a lot of emotion, a lot of tension. But what follows the battle according to Esther 9:17–19?

_____

_____

Was this celebration planned?

_____

_____

When you get through an anxious time and see what God has done, do you make a habit of stopping, resting, and celebrating the victory?

_____

_____

Celebration is seen all throughout Scripture. Here are just a few examples from one chapter in the Gospel of Luke. Record why and how the people in these parables celebrated:

LUKE 15:1–7 _____

_____

LUKE 15:8–10 _____

_____

Proverbs 11:10 tells us, "When it goes well with the righteous, the city _____, and when the wicked perish there are _____."

This is a good description of what's taking place here in Esther:

- Fasting has turned to feasting.
- Mourning has turned to joy and gladness.
- Fear has turned to boldness and confidence.
- Despair has turned to hope.

Once you've gone through the pain, the agony, the anguish, the waiting, and the spiritual battle, stop and take note of what God has done—and celebrate! Here are just a couple reasons to celebrate—fill in the remaining bullets with some reasons of your own:

- Celebrate to remember (Ex. 13:3).
- Celebrate His salvation (Isa. 25:9).
- 
- 
- 

What meaningful traditions and celebrations does your family have to acknowledge what God has done for you?

_____

_____

Regularly take time—individually and as a family—to celebrate the deeds of God. That's what Mordecai does. He institutes a Jewish Memorial Day of sorts. According to Esther 9, what is to be included in this day?

_____

_____

_____

_____

According to verse 26, what is this day to be called?

_____

_____

What is the significance of this name? (Look back at Week 3 if you need a refresher on the meaning of this word.)

_____

Read verses 26–28. Have the Jews kept this commitment?

_____

_____

There isn't just one proclamation but two. Who adds their vote to Mordecai's in verses 29–30?

_____

_____

As we seek to remember and celebrate the deeds of God, we anticipate that coming celebration when the battle will be completely over. God will triumph over all His enemies, and we will enter into eternal joy, feasting, and celebration.

List ways you can celebrate Christ's victory on a regular basis.

_____

_____

_____

# Day 5: Esther's "PS"

_Read Esther 10._

Esther 10 has just three verses. It's like a PS to the story.

Read the chapter, and record whose name surprisingly does not appear.

_____

Why do you suspect this person's name is missing from the conclusion of this story?

_____

_____

Esther has fulfilled the purpose for which God brought her into the kingdom "for such a time as this." Her story is really God's story.

How about you? Do you more often find yourself seeking a position of prominence or simply striving to be faithful to fulfill what God had called you to do?

_____

_____

Whose name surprisingly *is* made much of in this chapter?

_____

In the opening scene of this book, he wasn't even on the radar. He was a nobody.

How does our culture say you can get ahead?

_____

_____

Mordecai's life demonstrates a different way. Throughout the book of Esther, we don't see evidence that he aspired to be great in the eyes of men. But because of his servant's heart, God exalted him. You might think you can't win that way, but in God's economy, it's those who lay down their lives who ultimately "win."

Why was Mordecai both great and powerful (v. 3)? Because "he sought the _____ of his people and spoke _____ to all his people."

What does welfare mean?

_____

_____

What does peace mean?

_____

_____

You may not have as prominent a position as Mordecai has at the end of the book of Esther, but:

- What kind of leader are you?
- What kind of servant are you?
- If you have children or someone you manage at work, do you seek their welfare or your own?
- Do your words promote peace or discord?

Read Ephesians 6:5–9. While the culture in Paul's day included masters and servants, these principles are still true for those who have a subordinate position to you. What can you do to value these people? How can you communicate your respect for them?

_____

_____

_____

_____

Remember: Don't exalt yourself. Don't try to bring others down. Let God lift you up in His split-second timing for His purposes. Wait on the Lord.

*Back to the Beginning*

At the beginning of this study, we outlined seven truths we hoped would impact your life through the book of Esther.

- **You are in a battle.**
- **God has a sovereign plan.**
- **You are a part of God's plan.**
- **God's plan will never fail.**
- **It's a beautiful thing to live under God's caring providence.**
- **There is no situation so desperate God cannot redeem it.**
- **Don't judge the outcome of the battle by the way things look right now.**

These aren't just nice ideas to put in a flowery print and hang on your wall. They aren't simply sharable thoughts to make you feel good. They are *truth*. We can live differently knowing that the unseen hand of God is always at work for our good and His glory.

Choose one of these truths and write about how it will impact your view of God and your circumstances moving forward.

_____

_____

_____

_____

*A Blessing as You Go*

Our study of Esther has come to a close, but we trust the truth about God's providence that you have learned will deepen your love for Christ, your Deliverer, long past the close of this book.

A blessing from Romans 15:4–6 for you:

For whatever was written in former days was written for our instruction, that through endurance and through the encouragement of the Scriptures we might have hope. May the God of endurance and encouragement grant you to live in such harmony with one another, in accord with Christ Jesus, that together you may with one voice glorify the God and Father of our Lord Jesus Christ.

Amen.

# Week 1:

- Professor Dale Ralph Davis refers to God's providence as "that frequently mysterious, always interesting way in which Yahweh provides for his servants in their various needs." Discuss what you learned about God's providence in Week 1.

- How does Romans 8:28 help you trust that God's unseen hand is always working on your behalf? In your life, where is His hand most evident or least evident?

- What do you find helpful from Nancy's four questions to evaluate potentially enslaving behaviors on Day 2?

- Discuss the Scripture references from Exodus, Daniel, and Acts on Day 3. When is it right to disobey the authorities placed over us?

- After completing the first week of this study, how are you hoping Queen Esther's story helps you trust the story of your life God is writing?

# Week 2:

- Contrast God's way of viewing women with the world's way. How do Psalm 139:8–12 and Revelation 21:1–4 (Day 1) encourage you that while God doesn't always rescue us from peril, He is always redeeming and bringing about His purposes in His own way and time?

- In your own words, describe God's kingdom purposes for His children using the verses on page 26. Considering your own life, are there changes you want to make to fulfill God's purposes for you?

- How would you use the truths of Psalm 121:3–4 to encourage someone who is feeling alone and abandoned during a hard time? How are you personally encouraged?

- Living a life of greater simplicity and contentment like Esther is worth striving for. What would that look like in your present season of life?

- How were you encouraged through Proverbs 13:21, Matthew 16:27, and Galatians 6:7 (Day 5) that God ultimately rewards faithfulness? Were you able to apply these truths to a specific situation in your life right now?

---

# Week 3:

- Through studying the history of the Amalekites, we learned Haman wouldn't exist if Saul had fully obeyed the Lord. What are some consequences of partial obedience? Share specifics if you can.

- Can you tell about a time when you or someone you know had to go against others' advice in order to please God?

- Share how you identify with any of the "Haman" tendencies of controlling people and situations, grasping for power, or erupting with anger.

- How does knowing that Satan is a defeated foe give you renewed hope for a difficulty you're facing in the present or will face in the future?

- Brainstorm ways that you and your group members can live as upstanding citizens who influence your community for good. Use the Scripture references on page 43 as a basis for your discussion.

# Week 4:

- What are practical ways Christians can dress in humility, contrition, brokenness, and mourning over our sin?

- Which of the promises of Scripture found on page 56 is most encouraging for your life at this moment? Why?

- Esther came to a point of total abandon to God's will when she said, "If I perish, I perish" (Est. 4:16). What is God asking you to humbly surrender to His will right now? How does knowing Jesus is the "King of kings and Lord of lords" (Rev. 19:16) help you trust Him more?

- What did you learn from Esther's self-control, patience, and sensitivity in responding to her husband and God that you can apply to your life?

- What is your personal response to the snapshot of today's persecuted church? Take time as a group to pray for persecuted Christians to close your time together.

## Week 5:

- Are there situations in your life that seem to be going from bad to worse? What fresh hope do you gain by knowing that God often chooses to work in the darkest moments to show His power and glory?

- Mordecai could have been gripped by bitterness, but there's no evidence of it in his life. What damaging effects of bitterness have you personally experienced? How can Christians practically "put away" all bitterness (Eph. 4:31)?

- Can you share of a time in your life when you witnessed the split-second timing of God?

- Is discerning when to speak and when to be silent a challenge for you? What steps can we take to make the right choice?

- How does knowing "the way things are now is not the way they will always be" change how you view life? How were you comforted by the verses on page 76?

## Week 6:

- Is your prayer life rejuvenated by Esther's example in Esther 8:3–6? If so, how? What are your main obstacles to prayer? How should Christians be emboldened to approach the throne of grace with confidence (Heb. 4:16)?

- How often should we celebrate that Christ secured our freedom from sin and death through His sacrifice on the cross? Since our Deliverer has declared an edict of victory, how should this truth change the way we battle sin? (See Romans 7:24, 8:2.)

- How are you doing in your daily battle to fight against the world, the flesh, and the devil? Are there ways our group can come alongside you?

- Read Psalm 126:1–3. Take time to celebrate with each other the great things God has done in your life, family, or church. Share one example as briefly and specifically as you can.

- As you've studied Esther's story, how has your story come into a clearer focus? How have you grown in placing your hope and trust in God's providence as He orchestrates every detail of our lives and of this universe?

Listen in as women discuss this study in the Women of the Bible podcast by Revive Our Hearts. Find it at ReviveOurHearts.com/Esther.

# Notes

[1] Naim Dangoor, "The Jews of Iraq," *The Scribe*, Autumn 2001, http://www.dangoor.com/74034.html.

[2] "Persian Empire," History.com, A&E Television Networks, accessed January 14, 2019, https://www.history.com/topics/ancient-middle-east/persian-empire.

[3] Joshua J. Mark, "Susa," *Ancient History Encyclopedia*, accessed January 14, 2019, https://www.ancient.eu/susa.

[4] Sheena Tyler, "God's Providence and the D-Day Landings," *Evangelical Times*, September 2014, https://www.evangelical-times.org/20735/gods-providence-and-the-d-day-landings/, accessed January 22, 2019.

[5] Dale Ralph Davis, *1 Samuel: Looking on the Heart*, Focus on the Bible Commentaries (Fearn, Scotland: Christian Focus, 2000), 257.

[6] Nancy DeMoss Wolgemuth, *Adorned: Living Out the Beauty of the Gospel Together* (Chicago: Moody, 2017), 146–150.

[7] Herodotus, *The Histories*, trans. Robin Waterfield (New York: Oxford University Press, 1998), 7:28, 38–39.

[8] Ibid., 7:34–35.

[9] Ibid., 9:10–113.

[10] Mary A. Kassian, *Girls Gone Wise in a World Gone Wild* (Chicago: Moody, 2010), 65–66.

[11] Gerson B. Levi, Kaufmann Kohler, and George A. Barton, "Ahasuerus," Jewish Encyclopedia, accessed January 30, 2019, http://www.jewishencyclopedia.com/articles/967-ahasuerus/.

[12] Flavius Josephus, *Complete Works of Josephus*, vol. 2, 4 vols. (New York: Bigelow, Brown, n.d.), April 4, 2008, accessed January 30, 2019, https://archive.org/details/completeworksofj02jose/page/172/.

[13] Aaron Earls, "Quarter of a Billion Christians Face Major Persecution in 2018," Facts and Trends, January 29, 2018, https://factsandtrends.net/2018/01/29/quarter-billion-christians-face-major-persecution-2018/.

[14] Jeremy Weber, "'Worst Year Yet': The Top 50 Countries Where It's Hardest to Be a Christian," Christianity Today, January 11, 2017, https://www.christianitytoday.com/news/2017/january/top-50-countries-christian-persecution-world-watch-list.html.

[15] "What is the Meaning of Sackcloth and Ashes?" GotQuestions.org, January 09, 2019, accessed January 30, 2019, https://www.gotquestions.org/sackcloth-and-ashes.html.

[16] James Strong, *New Strong's Exhaustive Concordance*, King James Version ed. (Nashville: Nelson Reference & Electronic, 2005).

[17] Wikipedia, "Purim," accessed January 30, 2019, https://en.wikipedia.org/wiki/Purim.

[18] Wikipedia, "Victory in Europe Day," accessed January 30, 2019, https://en.wikipedia.org/wiki/Victory_in_Europe_Day.

[19] Wikipedia, "Victory over Japan Day," accessed January 30, 2019, https://en.wikipedia.org/wiki/Victory_over_Japan_Day.

# Reflections

# Reflections

MORE FROM

*Revive Our Hearts*™

RADIO • EVENTS • BLOGS

LEADERS

REVIVE OUR HEARTS . COM

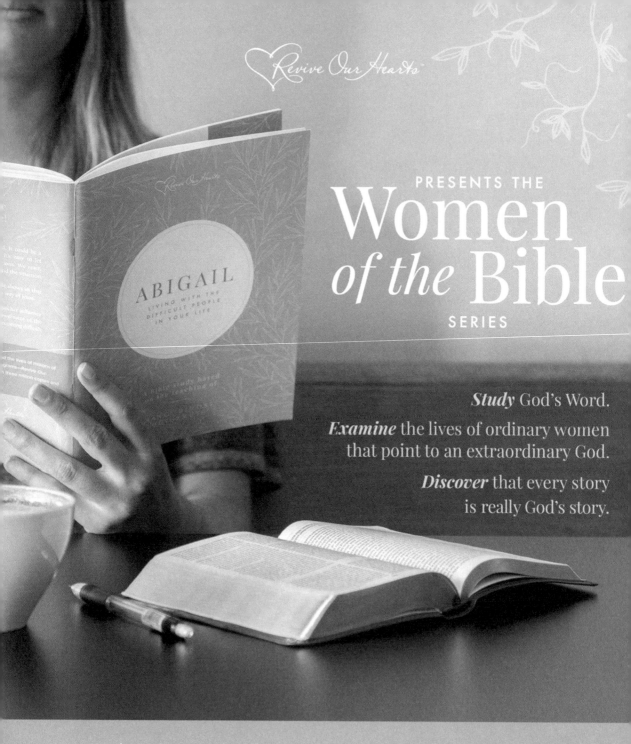